Lifestyles of the Rich & Faithful

Lifestyles of the Rich & Faithful

A Handbook for Successful Christian Living

By
Betty R. Price, D.D.

Faith One Publishing
Los Angeles, California

Lifestyles of the Rich & Faithful
A Handbook for Successful Christian Living
ISBN 1-883798-40-X
Copyright © 1999 by
Betty R. Price, D.D.
P.O. Box 90000
Los Angeles, CA 90009

Published by Faith One Publishing
7901 South Vermont Avenue
Los Angeles, California 90044

Table Of Contents

1

The Lifestyle of Success

As more Christians are exposed to the Word of Faith, we hear many reports of Believers receiving the supernatural abundance of God. This is exciting, but even in this biblically enlightened time, there are still too many people who profess the name of Jesus who are going without their needs being met. Why is this so? What is the problem within the Body of Christ that all of God's children are not receiving His best? We are told in the Bible that God is not a respecter of persons (Acts 10:34), and that He wants to bless all His children with abundance. So, there must be something that some of us are not doing that is hindering us from receiving the promised blessings of the Lord.

The Book of Proverbs tells us more than once that the reason why many people fail to receive God's best is because they live lifestyles that are contrary to His Word. These Believers expect to receive the promises, even though they have put themselves in positions *not* to receive them. In other words, they have cut themselves off from the Lord by their lifestyles. The Scriptures provide important instructions on how we are to live. But too many Christians are living any way they want and overlooking what the Word of God says. They do whatever their bodies tell them to do, and they entertain whatever thoughts come into their minds, yet the Bible says in 1 Thessalonians 4:4:

That each of you should know how to possess his own vessel [body] in sanctification and honor

This verse tells us that we, as children of God, are to live an honorable, sanctified lifestyle. This is how we position ourselves to receive the blessings of our heavenly Father. Notice that God tells us to possess our own vessels. In other words, He is not going to make us do it, nor will He do it for us. We have to will to do His Word—the decision is ours.

I remember counseling a woman who was living with a man as if they were married, when, in fact, they were not. She came to me because she found out that she had cancer. Naturally, she wanted to get better, and I suppose she was thinking that I could just pray and lay hands on her and all would be well. Then she could go right on living as though nothing had ever happened. I had to tell her that God could do nothing until she had separated herself from her immoral living condition. "Well," she asked, "doesn't God have mercy? Won't He have mercy and overlook this situation?"

This is the way a lot of Christians think. They rely on God's mercy, but they do not see the need to do what His Word says. We believe God is, and should be, there to protect and help us, but then we do not recognize our responsibility to do our best to walk upright before Him and the world. Some people think God just winks His eye and does not look at our sin. Many think God will honor us as long as we are doing what we believe is right. Those of us who think like this are being deceived. We can count on our heavenly Father to honor His Word, not on what we believe is acceptable behavior. And just because God does not strike us dead right while we are in sin does not mean that our sin is all right with God.

Galatians 6:7 says:

Do not be deceived, God is not mocked; for whatever a man sows, that he will also reap.

God is not mocked—we can be sure that our sin is going to catch up with us. So we should take His Word seriously; it is not to be made fun of or taken lightly. Verse eight goes on to say:

For he who sows to his flesh will of the flesh reap corruption, but he who sows to the Spirit will of the Spirit reap everlasting life.

The word *corruption* means "decay" and "death." You are sowing death in your life when you participate in sin. You should think of this before you enter into things that go against the Word of God. Sowing to the Spirit is obeying the Word of God, and it reaps everlasting life.

You may say, "Well, I'm a Christian. I already have life everlasting." But you will not have it in manifestation if your lifestyle is one of sinning, because sin cuts off the blessings of God. I cannot say this enough: God is not involved in any of our circumstances when we are involved in any kind of immorality or sin. Christians need to know that an unholy lifestyle keeps us from receiving from God, even though God wants so much to bless us.

For example, this lady felt that living with her boyfriend was okay because she said they were not sexually active. But she failed to realize that their living arrangement gave the appearance of sin, and the Bible says to **abstain from every form of evil** (1 Thessalonians. 5:22).

Some Believers think that since God wants to bless His children, we do not have to use our faith. What we have to understand is that the blessings of God are not automatic. There is an enemy who is standing in the way to block those blessings from coming through, and it is the force of faith that has to override the enemy to bring the promises of God to pass in our lives.

Living by faith, as the Word of God admonishes us, is supposed to be the lifestyle of the Believer.

Hebrews 11:6 tells us:

> **But without faith it is impossible to please Him [God], for he who comes to God must believe that He is, and that He is a rewarder of those who diligently seek Him.**

So, if it takes faith to please God now, then it always has and always will take faith to please Him, because God never changes. In fact, in Malachi 3:6, the Lord says that He does not change. So we have to use our faith to receive what God has in store for each of us. Satan, our enemy, is diligent and ever on his job, and the way to defeat him and keep him from stealing our blessings is by exercising our faith.

The bottom line is that if we are going to receive God's best, then we are going to have to start acting like children of God by living a lifestyle that is pleasing to Him. As He is holy, so must we live holy lives by separating ourselves from all sin and immorality. And just as our heavenly Father is a God of faith, we also must be people of faith by living according to His Word and not by how we feel, or what we think. The Lord is not obligated to answer our prayers or even to honor His Word in our lives if we are not living according to His instructions outlined in the Bible.

It is my heart's desire to see all in the Body of Christ prospering in the things of God. I am convinced that if we would do what the Word of God tells us to do, we, as Christians, will receive God's best and achieve the successful Christian lifestyle for which Jesus gave His all.

2

The Lifestyle of Holiness

In Leviticus 11:45, God tells the children of Israel:

> **For I am the Lord who bring you up out of the land of Egypt, to be your God. You shall therefore be holy, for I am holy.**

That was God's command to the Israelites, when He delivered them from Egyptian bondage, and it is still His command to every one of His children today.

Isaiah 6:1-3 says:

> **In the year that King Uzziah died, I saw the Lord sitting on a throne, high and lifted up, and the train of His robe filled the temple.**
>
> **Above it stood seraphim; each had six wings: with two he covered his face, with two he covered his feet, and with two he flew.**

> **And one cried to another and said:**
> **"Holy, holy, holy is the Lord of hosts;**
> **The whole earth is full of His glory!"**

This is referring to our heavenly Father. Notice the words, "Holy, holy, holy." There are just so many Scriptures in the Bible that refer to God's holiness that there is simply not enough room to cover them all, but for the sake of this study, let's look at one Scripture regarding God's holiness:

Psalm 99:9:

> **Exalt the LORD our God**
> **And worship at His holy hill;**
> **For the LORD our God is holy.**

As children of the Most High God and followers of the Lord Jesus Christ, we are expected to be holy and live lives that are above reproach. Personally, I don't believe the Body of Christ takes the concept of being *holy* seriously enough, because too many of us as Christians do not exemplify what Jesus exemplified when He walked the earth. Everything connected with God is referred to as being holy. Even His Word is referred to as the *Holy Bible.* The Church should be a holy place. Most important of all, our bodies should be holy places, because we are God's temple. And when we do not live holy lives, we are not living up to what He expects of us, and we cut off our blessings from Him.

The words *sanctify* and *sanctified,* which mean to set apart to a holy service, are similar to the word *holy.* However, *holiness* is the way we set ourselves apart, while *sanctify* or *sanctified* is the way God sets us apart. In other words, we cannot do anything to sanctify ourselves. God sanctifies us when we receive Jesus as our Savior and Lord, but we can live a *sanctified* life, and that is a lifestyle of holiness.

1 Corinthians 1:2 says:

> **To the church of God which is at Corinth, to those who are sanctified in Christ Jesus, called to be saints, with all who in every place call on the name of Jesus Christ our Lord, both theirs and ours.**

The minute you receive Jesus as Savior, you become a saint and are expected to live the sanctified life — in other words, set apart to a holy service. Sanctification is a place in God. It is a place we receive when we become born again. Living a lifestyle of holiness is not something that automatically happens. You have to train yourself to live holy. One of the ways of doing this is by taking yourself away from unholy places, unholy people, and unholy actions. You have to will to live a holy lifestyle because the flesh is tugging at you all the time to pull you away from holy things. You have to always remember that you are the custodian of your body, so it is up to you to keep your body in line.

In Romans 6:19-23, the Apostle Paul writes:

> **I speak in human terms because of the weakness of your flesh. For just as you presented your members as slaves of uncleanness, and of lawlessness leading to more lawlessness, so now present your members as slaves of righteousness for holiness.**

In other words, the way you train your body to be holy is to make your body a slave to do what you know is right at all times, just as you used to be a slave to sin and do wrong before you became saved. You make rules for yourself to only do things that are right.

> **For when you were slaves of sin, you were free in regard to righteousness.**
> **What fruit did you have then in the things of which you are now ashamed? For the end of those things is death.**
> **But now having been set free from sin, and having become slaves of God, you have your fruit to holiness, and the end, everlasting life.**
> **For the wages of sin is death, but the gift of God is eternal life in Christ Jesus our Lord.**

When we are out there living in an unholy manner — doing our own thing — sometimes we don't realize that there is a payday coming. Romans 6:23 says, **the wages of sin is death.** There is going to be a death of something — a friendship, a marriage, a family relationship, a job, or something. Sin pays a wage, and usually it is a wage of destruction. In the Sixth Chapter of Galatians, we are told that they who sow to the flesh will of the flesh reap corruption.

First Thessalonians 4:3 says:

> **For this is the will of God, your sanctification: that you should abstain from sexual immorality.**

Unfortunately, there are too many Christian who act as if they cannot read what is in the Bible, or they just overlook this Scripture and go on and do whatever they want—whatever their minds or their bodies tell them to do. If their bodies say they need sex, they go and have sex, regardless of the consequences.

When you ignore what the Bible says, you are living in an unholy state. The thing about it is no one but you can change the state you are in—you have to do it. That is your part in living a holy lifestyle. It is up to us to do what God tells us if we want to be pleasing to Him and receive the blessings He has in store for those who are obedient to His will.

Hebrews 12:14 says:

Pursue peace with all people, and holiness, without which no one will see the Lord.

When I read Scriptures like this, I want to do everything I can to stay right with God because I want to see the Lord. I do not want to be counted among those Christians who do not give attention to the way they live before the world. They continue gossiping, lying, stealing, causing strife, and fornicating. They have to be miserable on the inside.

Personally, I like to obey the Word of God just to have the peace that comes with being obedient to the Lord. There is a peace that passes all understanding when you are obedient to the Word. When you are not being obedient, you never feel free on the inside.

2 Corinthians 6:14-18 tell us:

Do not be unequally yoked together with unbelievers. For what fellowship has righteousness with lawlessness? And what communion has light with darkness?

11

And what accord has Christ with Belial? Or what part has a believer with an unbeliever?

And what agreement has the temple of God with idols? For you are temple of the living God. As God has said:

"I will dwell in them,
And walk among them.
I will be their God,
And they shall be My people."

Therefore
"Come out from among them,
And be separate, says the Lord.
Do not touch what is unclean,
And I will receive you."
"I will be a Father to you,
And you shall be My sons and daughters,
Says the Lord Almighty."

Verse 15 asks . . . **what accord has Christ with Belial?** We as Believers are considered Christ because we are the Body of Christ. Jesus is the head, and we are His body in the earth-realm. When you as a Believer go to bed with someone you are not married to, you put Christ in an unholy position. Just think about that! Anytime we are doing something that is wrong or sinful, Christ is there with us by the power of the Holy Spirit. He lives within us Believers. If we could just learn to see ourselves as Christ's representative and realize that every time we act in an unholy manner, someone is watching us and judging the Lord.

2 Corinthians 7:1:

Therefore having these promises, beloved, let us cleanse ourselves from all filthiness of the flesh and spirit, perfecting holiness in the fear of God.

God has given us so many wonderful and beautiful promises in His Word, and we claim those promises and expect them to come to pass in our lives when we act in obedience. And it is not hard to do; it is just a matter of making up our minds to follow the Lord. We may have to change the places we go, our friends, and even avoid family members. I am not saying to get away from a husband or a wife, because the Lord will certainly have to guide and help in a situation like that. But sometimes we may have to leave family and friends, particularly where there are no other Believers around, and where your spirit is constantly being vexed by association with them.

This is why it is so important to have a personal relationship with Jesus Christ. If you have to leave friends and family, it will not matter so much because we have the Number One Person with us. The key is that we really have to believe that Jesus is who He says He is and He is that to us. When you have that kind of relationship with the Lord, whatever anyone else does will not matter. Proverbs 16:7 says that when a man's ways please the Lord, He will make even his enemies to be at peace with him.

First Thessalonians 3:11-13 says:

Now may our God and Father Himself, and our Lord Jesus Christ, direct our way to you.
And may the Lord make you increase and abound in love to one another and to all, just as we do you.
So that He may establish your hearts blameless in

holiness before our God and Father at the coming of
our Lord Jesus Christ with all His saints.

We become established in the Lord as we obey His
Word. And when we show love one to another that, too, is
living in holiness, because we are obeying the Lord's command that we love one another as He has loved us.

Since God made us, why would we think His way is
hard? Doesn't He know what is best for us? It is that sinful
nature of disobedience that we all were born with that causes
the problem. We can change that nature. We just have to be
determined to live according to God's dictates and develop
our faith in the Word. That is why it is important to attend
a Bible-teaching, Bible-believing church — because, faith
comes by hearing and hearing by the Word of God.

Hebrews 12:5:

**And you have forgotten the exhortation which
speaks to you as to sons:**
*"My son, do not despise the chastening of the
Lord,*
*Nor be discouraged when you are rebuked by
Him;*
For whom the Lord loves, He chastens,
And scourges every son whom He receives."

God chastens or trains us by His Word. Often our
flesh does not want to do the Word and so we are chastened
until we learn our lesson. Our flesh rebels against God's
chastening, and some Christians fall into sin because their
flesh is rebelling.

Hebrews 12:10 states:

> **For they indeed for a few days chastened us**
> [talking about our earthly fathers] **as seemed best to**
> **them, but He for our profit, that we may be partakers**
> **of His holiness.**

God does not whip us, or, as some people think, put sickness and disease on us to chasten us. Sometimes, we do not want to hear what God tells us, because deep down we know when we are doing wrong. Our born-again spirits let us know.

A few years back, a couple of young women in our congregation got pregnant out of wedlock. One Sunday, my husband felt led to speak on the subject of fornication and its consequences. Later, one of the young ladies' mother called me and said that her daughter had come to church that Sunday and the pastor had talked about her publicly. She said that her daughter had gotten her feelings hurt and she was not going to return to the church.

Ironically, Fred [Price], my husband and pastor of the church, did not know anything about the young lady. In fact, he did not even know she was in the audience. But the girl was chastened by the teaching. That is how the Lord deals with us. He chastens us through the ministry gifts He has set in the Church, or through the Word.

It will be so wonderful when the Body of Christ gets itself together and on one accord by living and doing right. I believe that there is nothing on earth that God will not do for us when that happens.

Ephesians 4:22-24 states:

> **that you put off, concerning your former conduct**
> **the old man which grows corrupt according to the de-**
> **ceitful lusts,**

and be renewed in the spirit of your mind,
and that you put on the new man which was created according to God in true righteousness and holiness.

Again, we are reminded that it is our responsibility to live a holy life. As we diligently put on this new man — our Christian lifestyle — we become holy. As we take off the old man — our former conduct, the way we used to be — and walk according to the Word, we become like Jesus. The thing is you have to stay with it constantly. You cannot give up or get tired.

I know this sounds very difficult to do. Actually, it is not. It is just a matter of being determined to do the Word by allowing the Holy Spirit to guide and help train us.

First Peter 1:13-16 tells us:

Therefore, gird up the loins of your mind, be sober, and rest your hope fully upon the grace that is to be brought to you at the revelation of Jesus Christ;

as obedient children, not conforming yourselves to the former lusts, as in your ignorance;

but as He who called you is holy, you also be holy in all your conduct,

because it is written, "Be holy, for I am holy."

This is a commandment from God. And God would not tell us to do something we could not do, or be something we could not be. All through the Bible God is telling us how to live, because He knows the challenges we face in this life. If we keep hearing and studying the Word and then determine to be doers of that Word, then we will come to the point where we will live that holy lifestyle without even thinking about it.

When I learned that God has done everything He is going to do for us, as far as delivering us from the wiles of the devil, and that I had to mix my faith with the Word in order to receive the blessings of God, then I knew that it was up to me and not up to the Lord. So when things are not working for me, I do not ask God why. I just check myself out and find out what is going on.

If I know I have not done wrong and that I am right on the inside, I just wait on God. Sometimes it can be just an attack from the enemy, trying to get me to stop believing that God is going to do what He says He is going to do. Satan is not stronger than God. That is why I dare to stand on God's Word. Jesus has already provided healing and prosperity for us, and has taken care of all our needs. We merely have to learn how to get His promises to manifest in our lives, and the first step we have to take in that direction is to live a holy lifestyle.

Just think about it — Jesus gave His life so that we can walk in the fullness of God. We do not have the words in our vocabulary to adequately describe all that Jesus did when He died on the cross for us. Then He went into hell and served the penalty that had to be paid for our sins and our disobedience. When you think about God's love and the sacrifice He made by sending His Son to redeem us, and the price Jesus paid to make that redemption a reality, that should make us all want to do right and live holy.

Jesus said in John 14:21:

> **"He who has My commandments and keeps them, it is he who loves Me. And he who loves Me will be loved by My Father, and I will love Him and manifest Myself to him.**

Notice it says "to keep." That's how you can tell if you love Jesus — if you are being a doer (keeper) of the Word, and not just a hearer only. And then He says that if we love Him, we would be loved by the Father. If you want the Father to manifest Himself to you, then keep His Word. We always want God to do something for us. First, let's do what He says. Then when we do, He will show Himself strong on our behalf in a mighty way.

3

The Lifestyle of Righteousness

One of the ways to instill holiness in our lives is to fully understand the nature of our right-standing with God, which the Bible calls *"righteousness."*

While praying to His Father, Jesus says in John 17:25-26:

> **"O righteous Father! The world has not known You, but I have known You; and these have known that You sent Me.**
>
> **And I have declared to them Your name, and will declare it, that the love with which You loved Me may be in them, and I in them.**

Notice that Jesus calls the heavenly Father, **"O *righteous* Father."**

Vine's Expository Dictionary of Biblical Words gives this definition of the word *righteousness* as being "the character or quality of being right or just; it was formerly spelled *'rightwiseness,'* which clearly expresses the meaning. It is used to denote an attribute of God, e.g., Rom. 3:5, the context of which shows that 'the *righteousness of God'* means essentially the same as His faithfulness or truthfulness, that which is consistent with His own nature and promises; Rom. 3:25, 26, speaking of His 'righteousness' as exhibited in the death of Christ, which is sufficient to show men that God is neither indifferent to sin nor regards it lightly. On the contrary, it demonstrates that quality of holiness in Him, which must find expression in His condemnation of sin."

With regard to our righteousness in God through Christ, *Vine's* tells us that "all who have accepted Jesus Christ as Lord and Savior have been brought into right-standing with God ("justified" or "declared righteous") or into a right relationship with God. This righteousness is unattainable by obedience to any law, or by any merit of man's own, or any other condition than that of faith in Christ Jesus. The man who trusts in Christ becomes the *righteousness of God in Him* (II Corinthians. 5:21) i.e., becomes in Christ all that God requires him to be, and all that he could never be in himself."

We become brand-new when we are born-again, and we are commanded by the Word to grow up in the things of the Lord. That means we have to know what it is to be righteous or, rather, what it is to be in right-standing with God. The way to do that is to take off fleshly things and put on Christ Jesus — that is, put on a right way of living, a right way of thinking, and a right way of acting — which we call living the holy, sanctified life. As my husband writes in his book *Identified With Christ,* "Righteousness means the ability of you as a person to stand in the presence of God as free from sin and condemnation, as though there had never been any spiritual death in you from the time of your conception. It is as though you had never done anything wrong and were absolutely perfect." As we strive to live this life and be all that God would have us to be according to the Word, Psalm 84:11 becomes ours:

> **For the Lord God is a sun and shield;**
> **The Lord will give grace and glory;**
> **No good thing will He withhold**
> **From those who walk uprightly.**

When we, as Believers, see Scriptures like that, we should want to walk uprightly, recognizing what God has provided for us in Christ Jesus.

Isaiah 11:1-2 tells us:

> **There shall come forth a Rod from the stem of Jesse,**
> **And a Branch shall grow out of his roots.**
> **The Spirit of the Lord shall rest upon Him,**
> **The Spirit of wisdom and understanding,**
> **The Spirit of counsel and might,**
> **The Spirit of knowledge and of the fear of the LORD.**

All these attributes belong to the Christian. However, like *holiness,* they are not automatic. You have to find out first what Jesus is like and then be obedient to do what He tells you to do. You have to feed your spirit on the Word of Go so that you can grow up in Christ Jesus and be like Him.

Isaiah 11:3-5:

> His delight is in the fear of the LORD,
> And He shall not judge by the sight of His eyes,
> Nor decide by the hearing of His ears;
> But with righteousness He shall judge the poor,
> And decide with equity for the meek of the earth;
> He shall strike the earth with the rod of His mouth,
> And with the breath of His lips He shall slay the
> wicked.
> Righteousness shall be the belt of His loins,
> And faithfulness the belt of His waist.

We want to learn as much as we can about *righteousness,* so that we can be like little Christs walking the earth setting the captives free.

First John 1:9 tells us:

> If we confess our sins, He is faithful and
> just to forgive us our sins and to cleanse us from
> all unrighteousness.

We have to understand that when we sin, we lose our sense of righteousness. But if we confess our sins, God will immediately forgive us and put us back into right-standing with Him.

First John 2:1 says:

> My little children, these things I write to you, so
> that you may not sin. And if anyone sins, we have an
> Advocate with the Father, Jesus Christ the righteous.

Jesus is our advocate. He is the one who causes us to have this right-standing with God and forgiveness of our sins. Isn't that wonderful? Forgiveness all the time! And we, as Christians, should be just like our heavenly Father, always ready and willing to forgive one another.

Matthew 25:31-40 tells us how the righteous are supposed to act:

> "When the Son of Man comes in His glory, and all the holy angels with Him, then He will set on the throne of His glory.
>
> "All the nations will be gathered before Him, and He will separate them one from another, as a shepherd divides his sheep from the goats.
>
> And He will set the sheep on His right hand, but the goats on the left.
>
> "Then the King will say to those on His right hand, 'Come you blessed of My Father, inherit the kingdom prepared for you from the foundation of the world:
>
> 'for I was hungry and you gave Me food; I was thirsty and you gave Me drink; I was a stranger and you took Me in; I was naked and you clothed Me; I was sick and you visited Me; I was in prison and you came to Me."
>
> 'Then the righteous will answer Him, saying, 'Lord, when did we see you hungry and feed You, or thirsty and give You drink?
>
> 'When did we see You a stranger and take You in, naked and clothe You?
>
> 'Or when did we see You sick, or in prison and come to You?'

> **"And the King will answer and say to them, 'Assuredly, I say to you, inasmuch as you did it to one of the least of these My brethren, you did it to Me.' "**

Jesus is not here in the earth-realm. But we are to represent Him as His body. We are Jesus' representatives, and when we act like these Scriptures describe, we are acting on His behalf. We are acting out our right-standing with God. The Lord is counting on us, so whatever we do not do, will not get done.

This is how we grow up into righteousness — by being obedient to the Word of God and by doing those things Jesus would do if He were here on earth. That is why we need to live a holy life. We can then represent Him in the way He should be represented. That way, the world will see that Jesus is the *Way,* the *Truth,* and the *Life.* It is not very hard to live a righteous life. It is just a matter of our making up our minds to do it.

Let's look at some of the blessings that come with our righteousness:

2 Corinthians 5:21:

> **For He [God] made Him [Jesus] who knew no sin to be sin for us, that we might become the righteousness of God in Him.**

As I said before, because of all the sacrifices the Father and Jesus made for us, we should hold as sacred our right-standing with the Lord and always want to act in righteousness. I am sure we would not be so ready to give in to temptation if we would consider our righteousness in Christ when we are tempted to do our own thing. In fact, we should ask ourselves these questions when we are faced with the temptation to do something that is questionable:

(1) Can Jesus go here with me?
(2) Would Jesus do this with me?
(3) Can I involve Jesus with this?

Whatever we cannot involve Jesus in, we should not be doing ourselves. This is how we begin to grow up in the Lord and live in our righteousness.

I covered this Scripture in the chapter on *Holiness,* but it bears repeating. Righteousness, holiness, and sanctification are very closely related, but I want to review this Scripture in reference to our righteousness:

2 Corinthians 6:14-18:

> **Do not be unequally yoked together with unbelievers. For what fellowship has righteousness with lawlessness? And what communion has light with darkness?**
>
> **And what accord has Christ with Belial? Or what part has a believer with an unbeliever?**
>
> **And what agreement has the temple of God with idols? For you are the temple of the living God. As God has said:**
> **"I will dwell in them**
> **And walk among them.**
> **I will be their God,**
> **And they shall be My people."**
> **Therefore**
> **"Come out from among them**

And be separate, says the Lord.
Do not touch what is unclean,
And I will receive you."
"I will be a Father to you,
And you shall be My sons and daughters,
Says the LORD Almighty."

Notice the Apostle Paul says that the Christian *is* righteousness, and that is why the Holy Spirit, through Paul, tells us as Believers not to be unequally yoked or involved with unbelievers. We do not think alike, and we should not be joined together. This is not only in man-woman relationships, but other relationships, as well — friendships, business ventures, and financial arrangements, although one of the most difficult relationships is the marriage relationship where a Believers is linked up with an unbeliever.

It is very hard to try to reason with someone who is not a Christian and cannot understand Christian beliefs, such as tithing. I have seen both women and men — but mainly women — come out of such relationships so messed up that it took all they could do to hold on to their self-esteem and their belief in God's Word. I have known women to come out of these unequally-yoked relationships needing counseling both spiritually and psychologically. That is why it is so important to follow the direction of the Holy Spirit and the Word.

You cannot go into such relationships thinking you are going to change the other person. Most times it does not work. Many of the women I have talked to said they had been very good Christians, but their flesh and emotions got in the way, and they did not take heed to what they had been taught. They ended up still being alone, or wishing they were alone, dejected and depressed, all because they did not follow this Scripture on being unequally yoked.

To the single person, Jesus is the only One you really need. And if you would allow Him to, He will send the right mate to you. That is, if you want a mate. I have heard of some women who have married men just for what the men could give them, or because they wanted a daddy in the home for their children. Love, or being a Christian, had nothing to do with it. But even though I know there are some men who have been done in by women, most of the time, it is women who get the brunt of things, and it is women, most of the time, who are left with the children to raise by themselves. But with or without children, Jesus can send the right husband and father, if the woman would do things His way and not allow her flesh to dictate to her instead of her righteous spirit.

Isaiah 61:10 says:

> **I will greatly rejoice in the Lord.**
> **My soul shall be joyful in my God;**
> **For He has clothed me with the garments of salvation,**
> **He has covered me with the robe of righteousness,**
> **As a bridegroom decks himself with ornaments,**
> **And as a bride adorns herself with her jewels.**

Isn't that beautiful! He has covered us as Christians with the robe of righteousness. Because we are covered with the Lord's righteousness, we should not want to get His righteousness soiled by our lifestyles. The Bible is full of what we need to know and what we should do and should not do as the righteousness of God. What we should do is put on Christ Jesus—that is, do the Word!

The Apostle Paul writes in Philippians 3:7-10:

> But what things were gain to me, these I have counted loss for Christ.
>
> Yet indeed I also count all things loss for the excellence of the knowledge of Christ Jesus my Lord, for whom I have suffered the loss of all things, and count them as rubbish, that I may gain Christ
>
> and be found in Him, not having my own righteousness, which is from the law, but that which is through faith in Christ, the righteousness which is from God by faith;
>
> that I may know Him and the power of His resurrection, and the fellowship of His sufferings, being conformed to His death.

"That I may know Him" — I just love this Scripture. We know Him by putting on His righteousness and not operating in our own so-called righteousness. That is what many Christians do. Yes, they are saved, but they follow their own rules of conduct rather than obedience to the Word. That is why the Church has not yet made a real impact on the world. There are still too many Christians who are not living in righteousness.

Proverbs 15:28-29 says:

> The heart of the righteous studies how to answer,
> But the mouth of the wicked pours forth evil.
> The Lord is far from the wicked,
> But He hears the prayer of the righteous.

If you want the Lord to hear your prayers, you have to live a righteous lifestyle. We should be making well-thought-out decisions for our lives. Yes, sometimes we make wrong decisions, because we are not perfect, but we should give thought to our actions and line our actions up with the Word.

Proverbs 18:10 tells us:

> **The name of the Lord is a strong tower;**
> **The righteous run to it and are safe.**

Isn't that a wonderful promise? We run to it and we are secure — because we are the righteousness of God. But if we are not acting righteously, the devil will take advantage of us every time.

Proverbs 28:1:

> **The wicked flee when no one pursues,**
> **But the righteous are as bold as a lion.**

When people are doing wrong, they are always afraid. They are always looking over their shoulders, always doing things under cover. But we can be bold when we are walking as righteous people walk, because we know God is on our side, and He will take care of us. We don't care what anyone tries to do to us. We just go on and count it a joy and a blessing when we are being persecuted for righteousness' sake. We can be bold and stand strong in the Lord.

God's Word is what gives me strength. Any time I hear something negative being said about me or my family, I just get stronger in the Lord and find more good things to do because I know the wicked will be taken care of. But the righteous can stand bold. God has promised us He will never leave us, and that the angels of the Lord encamp around and about us because we reverence and fear the Lord. When we have enough of the Word in us, we can stand and face anything. Yes, negative things will come against us because we live in a negative world. The Bible says, **Many are the afflictions of the righteous, but the Lord delivers him out of them all** (Psalm 34:19).

Psalm 45:6-7 says:

> **Your throne, O God, is forever and ever;**
> **A scepter of righteousness is the scepter of Your kingdom.**
> **You love righteousness and hate wickedness;**
> **Therefore God, Your God, has anointed You**
> **With the oil of gladness more than Your companions.**

This is referring to Jesus. We can choose to live the righteous life that God has for us, or we can choose not to. It is all up to us.

4

The Lifestyle of Faith

People miss out on getting their needs met or answers to their prayers because they lack faith in the heart. One of the reasons Christians do not have faith for everything God has for them is because they have not yet learned to apply to their total way of living the Romans 10:10 faith formula, which states:

> **For with the heart one believes unto right-eousness, and with the mouth confession is made unto salvation.**

Verse 10 is the formula for receiving whatever you need from God, not just salvation. For example, with the heart one believes unto his needs being met, and with the mouth confession is made unto his needs being met. Belief and confession work hand in hand.

Romans 10:17:

> **So then faith comes by hearing, and hearing by the word of God.**

There should be more Christians prospering than there are. I think the major problem is that most Christians do not understand how faith works, or that faith without works is dead faith.

Many Christians fail in their walk because they have not actually been taught how to apply the Word to their lives. They hear words quoted from the Scriptures, but when it comes to understanding the Word of Faith, they miss it. Many of them try to confess and believe what little they hear taught, but their faith does not go anywhere, because faith comes by hearing, hearing, hearing, and hearing the Word taught. After a while, they become discouraged and give up, saying, "That faith stuff doesn't work!" Another problem is that some Christians confess the Word and say they believe it, but they live any kind of way.

Another problem is that some Christians say they are believing God for their finances, healing, and other things that would enhance their lives, but they do not think about believing God to get jealousy, envy, strife, and prejudice out of their hearts. They do not understand that it all has to work in line with the Word to receive from God.

Proverbs 4:20 tells us:

> **My son, give attention to my words;**
> **Incline your ears to my saying;**
> **Do not let them depart from your eyes;**
> **Keep them in the midst of your heart.**

> **For they are life to those who find them,**
> **And health to all their flesh.**
> **Keep your heart with all diligence.**
> **For out of it spring the issues of life.**

John 14:21 [Jesus is speaking]:

> **"He who has My commandments [His Word] and**
> **keeps them [does the Word], it is he who loves Me. And**
> **He who loves Me will be loved by My Father, and I will**
> **love him and manifest Myself to him."**

This verse alone should be enough to make you want to get into the Word. If you want to know if you love Jesus or not, you can test yourself by asking, *"Do I have Jesus' Word in my heart and do I keep it?"* You don't have to feel anything. According to the above Scripture, the way you know you are loved by the Father is to do the Word. You want Jesus to manifest Himself in your life? Then keep His commandments.

Sometimes we get so busy doing our daily jobs that we put studying the Word off until the last minute, or not do it at all. We forget that it is the Lord who is giving us the strength and the knowledge to do our jobs. The devil will have you doing all kinds of things to keep you from your study. You have to be determined to study. I don't care if you have to read the same Scripture ten times over; stick with it and beat the devil at his game, which is to cause you to be distracted. He knows that you can defeat him with the Word. You cannot go by how you feel. You have to learn how to walk by the Word of God if you want to defeat Satan and have success in life.

The more you study the Word, the more you will confess it; the more you confess it, the more your faith will grow.

The way I study the Bible is to go through the New Testament from Romans to Jude and underline all the Scriptures that tell me what God has provided for me as His child through Jesus. Then I memorize those Scriptures to get them into my spirit, so that when the issues of life come against me, I have the Word to fight with. We can't always get to the Bible to find a Scripture when we need it; that is why it is so important to take time to learn the Scriptures when you are well and strong and all your needs are met.

Ephesians 3:14-16 [this is the Apostle Paul speaking]:

> **For this reason I bow my knees to the Father of our Lord Jesus Christ,**
> **from whom the whole family in heaven and earth is named,**
> **that He would grant you, according to the riches of His glory, to be strengthened with might through His Spirit in the inner man.**

For you to be strengthened with might through His Spirit in the inner man means that you have to spend time praying in the Spirit, so you can build up your inner man. The Holy Spirit will be there to strengthen you. Faith does not work automatically. There are some things you have to do, and you cannot go by how you feel. You may not feel like praying in the Spirit, but you have to ignore your feelings if you want to get results. You have to develop a habit of praying in tongues, just as most people have developed habits of brushing their teeth, taking baths, and exercising. Many people do not enjoy exercising, but those of us who are committed to exercising do it because of the results we get. So if you want to be strengthened with all might in the inner man, you have to do your spiritual exercises consistently, just as you do physical exercises to get the desired results.

Ephesians 3:17-19 [this is the Apostle Paul speaking]:

that Christ may dwell in your hearts through faith; that you, being rooted and grounded in love,
may be able to comprehend with all saints what is the width and length and depth and height —
to know the love of Christ; that you may be filled with all the fullness of God.

In order for us to be filled with all the fullness of God, we have to let all the goodness and righteousness of God be a part of our lives. In all the fullness of God, there is no hate, prejudice, envy, jealousy or strife. God does not have any of that junk in Him. And yet we see these things manifested over and over in Christians. I think people do things because God doesn't come and strike them down right now. But you know why God does not do it? Because He has all the time in the world. I always encourage those who are not living right to get right immediately. You cannot play with God and think you are getting away with it because nothing bad has happened yet.

I hear stories all the time about ministers having had affairs almost all of their ministry lives, and because they have not been struck down they think they are getting away with it. God has time. The Bible says that our sin will find us out. If we want to receive God's best, we have to let faith dwell in our hearts. When the Bible says do not commit adultery, do not commit fornication, do not steal or lie, do not have envy or jealousy in our lives, and we follow these warnings, that is how faith dwells in our hearts. When we put faith in our hearts, then we will reap the benefits of God's promises.

Get busy doing what the Lord says and whatever needs we have will be taken care of. There is a Scripture in the Bible for whatever we may be facing. With faith in our hearts — and obedience to the Word — we will come through.

The Faith That Heals

By faith, we can overcome any situation we face in life. We have God's Word on it.

First John 5:4 tells us:

**For whatever is born of God overcomes the world.
And this is the victory that has overcome the world—
our faith.**

But this Scripture is true only when God's Word is real to us. We cannot be "hoping and praying" that God's Word will work in certain situations, and expect to be victorious in this life. We need to know the Word works — and that it works for us. We need to be ready to use the Word of God in the challenges we face, because it is our faith that brings God's promises to pass in our lives.

When I was diagnosed with lymphoma, I was prepared to fight the good fight of faith, because I had already put the Word to work in my life. More than 26 years ago, I used the Word to overcome fear. That was my first big victory, and ever since then I have been using God's Word to overcome every challenge in life. As soon as my leg began to ache, I started confessing God's Word over the discomfort. When I noticed my leg was really swollen, I called for the doctor and went right on declaring that by Jesus' stripes I was healed (1 Peter 2:24). When it was recommended that I be hospitalized, my husband and I immediately got into agreement (Matthew 18:19) that I was healed because, "He Himself took our infirmities ands bore our sicknesses" (Matthew 8:17). I was sure to do everything I knew to do in the natural, while keeping my confession and attitude in line with God's Word.

I gave the Word of God precedence over all the circumstances concerning my healing. As a result, I was anxious for nothing. I did not become discouraged, even though I was hospitalized for more than a week while the doctors put me through test after test. I had to undergo major surgery just so the doctors could diagnose the condition, yet I did not worry or have any fear. The results from the biopsy of the tumor found in my pelvic area were the worst news you could ever receive in your life, but I was not devastated. I knew to keep my trust in Him. See, my trust was already in Him — I just had to keep it there. So I was prepared.

This is why the command "to be doers of the word and not hearers only, deceiving yourselves" is given in James 1:22. We are never going to know the Word works until we do it. No matter how many Scriptures we hear, we will not benefit from them until we apply them. But as we step out in faith and begin doing the Word, we will see God's will come to pass. With each victory, our faith will grow until it is so strong that there is no challenge it cannot overcome — even cancer.

But far too many Christians are actually self-deceived. They do not see a need to think about God's Word until they are desperate. They believe they can develop their faith if and when they need it. You are deceived if you think you are not going to need your faith at some point in your life — and when you are desperate is not the time to begin developing it. You do not want to wonder if God's Word will work when you are battling cancer. You should not be hoping faith will work when you are facing foreclosure, or your children need food, clothing and shelter. You do not want to wait until you are in trouble to prove that God's Word is true. You have to know God keeps His Word the very minute the enemy comes to kill, steal, and destroy.

Far too many Christians have deceived themselves into thinking they can just believe for a miracle. Nowhere in the Bible does God guarantee miracles. You cannot count on a miracle, or on the gifts of the Spirit to be in manifestation, simply because you are in need. God does not respond to need; He responds to His Word. Only faith guarantees you the victory; so there are going to be times when you will have to use your faith.

When the doctors told me I needed chemotherapy followed by radiation, I wanted a miracle. I went for eight months and never received one. The tumor seized this opportunity to grow larger and larger. It grew so big I could not even walk! When I read the Gospel accounts of Jesus healing the sick, I noticed how many of the people received the manifestation of their healing after they took some action, some step of faith. You have to think about that when you are faced with certain situations. Faith is an action. There are some things you may have to do, that you do not want to do.

When you are facing your biggest challenges, all the discipline and training that comes with being a doer of the Word goes to work for you. Because I already knew the Word would work for me, Satan could not get me to question the validity of God's Word. I had already trained myself to speak in line with God's Word, so I did not have a challenge holding fast the confession of my faith without wavering. Since I knew the Scriptures, I knew I did not have to go searching for the promises that guaranteed my healing. I had my sword of the Spirit (Ephesians 6:17) ready. I instantly refuted the bad report Satan wanted to bring to pass in my life. I was well able to cast down the negative thoughts and imaginations Satan shot into my head. So I never fell prey to anxiety, worry, or doubt. I never had any fear. I experienced the blessed peace and assurance of God despite what all the doctors and the circumstances had to say.

People complain that faith does not make sense. Well, fear does not make any sense either! If you allow yourself to become afraid, what good does it do you? Satan will have you running around scared. Fear will kill you a lot faster than any sickness or disease. Faith, however, is giving the Word of God precedence over anything that exalts itself above the knowledge of God. Despite how grim the doctor's report may be, God says by Jesus' stripes you were healed (1 Peter 2:24). You can either believe God's Word and receive your healing by faith, or you can surrender to fear and death.

In John 10:10, Jesus lets us know that Satan is a thief. If he cannot rob you of your health and life, he will try to steal your peace and joy. There are people who have been healed, yet are scared that the sickness or disease that attacked them before is going to come back. What peace and joy is in that? I refuse to be afraid. My trust is in the Lord. He said He would satisfy me with long life (Psalm 91:6), so I believe as long as I have done all that I am supposed to do, there is no way Satan can hurt me.

In Psalm 112:7, it says **I will not be afraid of evil tidings because my heart is steadfast, trusting in the Lord.** If you trust in the Lord, then you have to bring the Scriptures to bear in your life when you are going through the fire and the water.

Many people do not stand against cancer. You hear all the time about people who just give in and die because they do not want to do what the doctor says. They think it is too hard. They forget that nothing is too hard for God. He said He would never leave you nor forsake you. He is right there with you to help you overcome any challenge you may be facing. He said in His Word He would make a way of escape (1 Corinthians 10:13).

I was at peace through both the chemotherapy and radiation treatments because I knew God was with me (Hebrews 13:5). There were times when I thought I could not make it through another minute, but God carried me through all the treatments — and right on schedule! I never had to miss a treatment because my blood count was low. In fact, the nurses and doctors were always amazed by how strong my blood remained throughout the treatments.

God is no respecter of persons (Acts 10:34); what He has done for me He will do for you. But until you have proven for yourself that God's Word works, you will never be able to step out in the faith that makes you a victorious overcomer. The more experienced you are at walking in line with God's Word, the easier it will be to successfully apply your faith when you are under attack. For your own well-being, become a doer of the Word. Do not wait until you need strong faith to begin exercising your faith muscles. Start now. Then when circumstances arise to challenge your very life, you will be prepared. Your faith will overcome even the world.

5

The Lifestyle of Peace

Even though Galatians 5:22 tells us that peace is a fruit of the re-created human spirit, there are still quite a few Christians who are not experiencing peace or joy in their Christian walk. In John 14:27 Jesus said:

> **Peace I leave with you, My peace I give to you; not as the world gives do I give to you. Let not your heart be troubled, neither let it be afraid.**

We are the ones who must keep our hearts from being troubled. And since Jesus told us to do so, that means we can. The Lord would never tell us to do anything we could not do. Jesus tells us in John 16:33:

> **These things I have spoken to you, that in Me you may have peace. In the world you will have tribulation; but be of good cheer, I have overcome the world.**

You may be going through trials and tribulations right now, but Jesus has already overcome those situations in your life. So you have to determine that you are going to walk in the peace He has provided, no matter what. If you do not make that determination, you will be up and down all the time, because there is rarely a time when you will not have an opportunity to have your peace taken away from you. As soon as you get through with one thing, there is something else to confront you. You are going to have to know that the end is good, and you have the victory.

In a family situation, one of the most common robbers of peace is discord in the husband/wife relationship. Sometimes, for various reasons, a couple just cannot get along. Then there is the parent/child relationship, where there is almost constant miscommunication. Perhaps, a daughter has gotten pregnant out of wedlock or a son is on drugs. Or, maybe there is a serious illness with a family member that is putting a financial and emotional strain on the rest of the family. All these circumstances can be robbers of your peace and joy in the Lord. But no matter what the situation, the Bible says in 1 Peter 5:7:

> **Casting all your care upon Him, for He cares for you.**

God made us all, so He knows exactly what we are going through. That is why He has given us His Word. If we will look at His Word and not at the situation, we will come out on top.

While I was going through my battle with cancer, if I had looked at what I was in, I would have never come out of it. I looked at the end and saw myself whole and healthy. Don't ever look at how you feel, or what you see. Only look at what you believe. I believe that I am healed by Jesus' stripes and what God says He will do in His Word.

A primary reason that peace is not more evident in the lives of many Christians is unforgiveness. Often, people do not forgive themselves, nor do they forgive others. They don't realize that while they are holding onto unforgiveness, they are hindering God's blessings. If you cannot forgive, God cannot forgive you. It is as simple as that.

Another reason for a lack of peace is loneliness. So many Christians waste their time dwelling on how lonely they are instead of getting busy giving to others and doing what they know to do. It is such a blessing to get involved in helping others. And it is a sure way to find peace.

Peace and Harmony in the Home

There are times when I am counseling women regarding situations in their marriage and my heart just goes out to them. I try to help them understand that if they would do the Word and have confidence in God, they would get the help they need, and things would turn out all right. Many times I hear, them say, "Yes, but I have tried that and it didn't work." These poor hurting women can not seem to understand that that is the problem — *they tried it.* They did not do the Word, because the Word works.

God did not lie to us; we have to believe what He said and act on that belief. If my husband and I had not decided long ago to do things the way we believe Jesus wanted us to do them, I do not know if we would be together today. We faced many of the same challenges that many couples face at some time or other in their marriage.

Many people have heard about the early struggles we had with our finances, but we had other challenges as well. Fred and I did not always see eye to eye on everything, including sex. But I had made up my mind that if the marriage did not work, it would not be my fault. When two people come together, they have to understand that they are different people, with different opinions and likes and dislikes — even though they love each other. And when a problem arises, someone has to yield. The Lord does not take sides; He will confirm the one who is right. Just make sure you are doing what you are supposed to do, then trust the rest to the Lord.

Some might say that is easier said than done. But how do you know whether or not it will work unless you do it? I know from experience that the Lord will work things out. There were times when my husband thought he was right about a certain matter, and I disagreed. I had made up my mind that I was not going to waste my time fussing and arguing with anyone. I don't think that is what marriage is about. I would simply tell him what I thought, and then I would go on with what was expected of me as a wife. I let God speak to my husband.

If you believe that God loves you and wants what is best for you, then know that He will work on your behalf, including ministering to your spouse. It is during these times that you will have a good opportunity to develop your faith and confidence in the Lord and His Word.

Sometimes things get messed up in a relationship because people want their way so badly that they end up fussing, complaining and nagging. Their spouses cannot even hear God speaking to them. If they were quiet, God could speak and their spouses could hear.

God ordained marriage, and He wants it to be a peaceful, loving relationship. And it can be that way, but couples have to grow up in their marriages, and age has nothing to do with it. There are some people who have been married for a long time and are of an age to know better, but still need to grow. The best way to grow in any area of living is to create a oneness with Jesus Christ. Once you know who you are in Christ, you can handle anything, but you have to grow.

Fred and I made it through more than 46 years of marriage by putting Jesus at the center of our relationship. If you do that, you will not mistreat one another and you will not do anything to one another that Jesus would not do. The Bible says in Galatians 6:9 not to grow weary while doing good, for in due season we shall reap if we do not lose heart. If you lose heart, you may never reap. So do not be weary in being kind, considerate, thoughtful, patient, and ready to give in, if necessary.

Many times people let a spirit of pride come in and steal peace from the home. You cannot have a peaceful home if there is constant arguing and fighting and everyone is trying to get his or her own way. Someone has to give in. What does it matter who gives in first, as long as peace is kept in the home? I am not saying that peace should be kept at all cost, if it means that giving in will cause a husband or wife to get out of the will of God. But most often that is not the case; it is simply people wanting to have their own way, and God has nothing to do with it.

Learn to turn those argumentative situations over to the Lord and believe that He will take care of things. Even when you know you are right, that will not convince a spouse — particularly if he or she has made up their minds that they are right. In situations like that, you are going to have to believe God that once you have spoken to your spouse, God will be working on him or her from that point on, helping them to see the right way. I know this is not easy to do, because people tend to want to keep picking up their problems instead of letting them remain with the Lord. Too often, we want God to solve the issue a certain way, and we want our spouses to act a certain way. But if we have truly given the situation over to the Lord, we should be at peace. If we trust our lives to the Lord, we certainly can trust our spouses to Him.

My advice, simply, is to be what you are supposed to be as a Christian, and God will take care of everything around you. Believe that and make that your daily confession. I have learned from personal experience, as well as from the Word and from observing others, that God and the Word will work on our behalf if we are doing what we are supposed to do.

6

The Lifestyle of the Family

In Ephesians 5:25, Paul tells us:

Husbands, love your wives, just as Christ also loved the Church and gave Himself for her.

If a man wants to know how to treat his wife, all he has to do is examine how Jesus treats the Church. I have never seen Jesus slap down the Church, and I do not believe there is any reason whatsoever for husbands to beat their wives. If a wife is a Christian, she is a member of the Body of Christ. So, when a husband strikes his wife, he is in essence hitting Christ. Just think about that!

In Verses 28-29, Paul adds:

So husbands ought to love their own wives as their own bodies; he who loves his wife loves himself.
For no one ever hated his own flesh, but nourishes and cherishes it, just as the Lord does the church.

God has placed the man as the head of the home. Now, he is not the god of the home. No woman should worship her husband. But God has placed man to be the caretaker, provider and protector of his wife and their children, just as Jesus is the caretaker, provider, and protector of the Church.

Our children's faith comes from teaching them God's Word by precept and example. Second Timothy 1:5 says:

> **When I call to remembrance the genuine faith that is in you, which dwelt first in your grandmother Lois and your mother Eunice, and I am persuaded is in you also.**

Timothy was a man of faith, but it started with his grandmother and mother. So the Word of God shows us that parents and even grandparents have an impact on their children.

We can see in Titus 2:1-6 how we are to raise our children.

> **But as for you, speak the things which are proper for sound doctrine:**
> **that the older men be sober, reverent, temperate, sound in faith, in love, in patience:**
> **the older women likewise, that they be reverent in behavior, not slanderers, not given to much wine, teachers of good things —**
> **that they admonish the young women to love their husbands, to love their children,**
> **to be discreet, chaste, homemakers, good, obedient to their own husbands, that the word of God may not be blasphemed.**

Likewise, exhort the young men to be sober-minded.

We are to teach our children by speaking sound doctrine, setting the example and giving specific instruction. Our older men of faith are charged with setting the example, but our older women of faith are also told to give instruction.

The older women are told to teach the younger women to love their children. Wouldn't you think loving your children would be automatic? Love is more than just a word or an emotion; it is an action. It is training your children to be clean and neat, giving them an education, and caring for them. Love is not giving your children everything they want, because Proverbs 22:15 tells us that foolishness is bound up in the heart of a child. That is why Proverbs 23:13–14 says not to withhold correction from our children, that the rod will deliver him or her from hell. So if a child needs a whipping, you had better whip him or that foolishness will stay in him. Children will do what comes naturally, often times what comes naturally is foolishness.

Older women are also to teach the younger women to be discreet. *Discreet* means "to curb your natural desires and emotions." If children are taught to be discreet while they are growing up, their parents will still be able to talk to them when they are teenagers. There is nothing our children won't learn or hear about out in the world. So, we must teach them to control their emotions and desires. We have to set rules for them and live the standard of the Word of God. I have constantly told my children that I do not care what they see done out there in the world; we follow the Word of God.

Another word I would like to point out is *chaste.* Chaste means to be "morally and sexually pure in thought and action." A lot of times mothers don't teach their children why chastity is so important; they just tell their girls, "Don't go around those boys." But that does not mean anything to a child. We must teach our children the truth about intimacy from Day One. We have to keep talking with them, so that the influences of the world do not outweigh the standards we have set at home. I tell my son, "We, as Christians, don't have sex before marriage. We wait." When my son was a teenager, we set rules for him. If he wanted to go out with a girl, then he had to double date with either my husband and me or with one of his sisters and her husband.

Our young women need to be taught to be keepers of the home. They need to keep their homes clean, neat and presentable. There is no greater task, responsibility, or privilege than to make a home for a family. Homemaking is a career. Some women look down on that, but it is important because the homemaker is charged with raising good citizens for the Kingdom of God.

A lot of women put their professions before their families. It is not good for our children to see their mothers neglecting them or their fathers. God's order is for the wife to care for her husband and then her children. It is okay for women to work, because they have talents and abilities, but they must be sure to believe God for a good baby-sitter. Women, make sure your children are cared for and take time to be a wife. Being a mother and a homemaker is a full-time job, so husbands should help if they need their wives to work outside of the home. If a woman's husband is expecting her to help him with the family income, then she should be able to expect him to help her with the household chores.

When my children were young, I stayed at home, but when they got older and I was able to help in the ministry,

I put that principle into practice. I said, "Whoever gets out of bed last should make it up"; so my husband started making the bed.

Titus 2:5 also says to teach our young women to be good. We have to be taught to be good. *Good* means to be kind, caring, not idle nor a gossiper or a busybody. We never know whom we are affecting by our idle talk. We have Christians who come to church to gossip, and they end up running people off with their gossip. Talking about people is not acting in love, or being good and kind. Women gossip so easily; it starts when they are young, fussing over boys and all kinds of things. So mothers need to teach their children that Christians do not gossip.

Our older women also need to teach the young women to be obedient to their husbands. Submission is not a bad word; it does not mean your husband is better than you. Submission means to yield; it has to do with function and order. I have a role, and my husband has a role. In a marriage relationship, someone has to yield and God ordained that women fulfill that role. But when a wife thinks her husband is not right, she should always tell him. If he does not agree, she should talk to the Lord, who is above her husband, and let Him handle her spouse. When the husband submits to God, and his wife submits to him, their children are usually well adjusted.

And being submitted does not include doing anything that is outside the Word of God. Wives are not required to submit to abuse. Our bodies are temples of the Holy Spirit; we are responsible for those bodies. Christ did not treat His church that way, so no woman should stay in a situation where someone is beating or abusing her.

If we want our children to be successful, we must start with ourselves. Our children need to see the Word operating in us, making us win in life. That lets them know that the Bible is relevant — a "now" book which can also lead them to victory. The sooner they learn this, the sooner they will be about their Father's business. They will know that everything they could ever try to do on their own will not amount to anything anyway. There is a verse of a song that goes, *"Only what is done for Christ will last."* If we can get this into our children while they are young and teach them to walk by faith, we can raise some real giants in God for the generations to follow.

Successful Intimate Relationships

When Paul tells husbands and wives in 1 Corinthians 7:5, **Do not deprive one another,** he means not to deprive one another of each other's body. The wife owes her body to her husband, and the husband owes his body to his wife. Paul tells us:

> **Do not deprive one another except with consent for a time, that you may give yourselves to fasting and prayer.**

This means that you cannot just suddenly decide that "I am going to fast and pray tonight and be alone." No, you have to ask and get consent from your spouse. A wife giving her body to her husband in an intimate way is the wife's responsibility, because Paul writes in 1 Corinthians 7:4:

> **Let the husband render to his wife the affection due her, and likewise also the wife to her husband.**

It is God's will that husbands and wives enjoy an intimate sexual relationship. This is one of the reasons He ordained marriage. Unfortunately, not all couples enjoy their sexual relationship and there are many reasons why this is the case. A primary reason is because a husband or wife (or sometimes both) may not know what to do to enjoy a good sex life. You do not automatically know what pleases your spouse when you first get married. You have to get to know one another. So you and your mate need to exercise patience with one another, and communicate your desires and feelings openly to speed this process along. Sex is a learning experience that develops with good communication.

Another reason many married couples do not enjoy a good sex life — and here I am mainly talking about the wife — is that her husband is constantly criticizing her. Her husband may put her down, and act cruel to her. Most of the time, a woman will rebel by withholding sex. Men, however, are different. You can say almost anything to a man, and he can forget it and still go to bed and want to have sex. But a woman may continue hurting for a long time from what is said to her. That is why a husband needs to be sensitive to what he says to his wife and how he says it. When a wife is hurt by something her husband has said, she should take an opportune time to let him know *before* they come together so they can get the air cleared between them.

Insecurity may also affect a woman's sex life. When finances are not right, or the husband has spent money unnecessarily at the wrong time, that tends to affect a woman's time of intimacy. When a wife is thinking, "The children need this, we need that, and there just is not enough money to go around," her mind is going to be on the family finances rather than on sex.

But this sense of security that wives need is not entirely financial, either. Sometimes, a husband will spend his time with his friends, and not with her. Sometimes, the husband is involved in adultery. Sometimes, he will compliment other women and not compliment her, so the wife does not feel loved. There is nothing wrong with complimenting other women, but a husband should also compliment his wife.

Also, some men do not share with their wives how they can look the very best for them. A man should encourage his wife to look her best and let her know that he appreciates her efforts to be her best for him.

Another reason a couple may not have a good sexual relationship is because of guilt. There can be something in a woman's past, such as premarital sex that may have led to an abortion, and the wife will carry that guilt over into the marriage. Sometimes such a situation can also affect a man's sexual relationship with his wife. In such cases, they need the Word of God. They need to understand that God forgives any sin a person commits once the person has repented and asked His forgiveness.

Another reason for a poor sexual relationship is that the wife may have too much responsibility. If both spouses work, or the wife is the only one working, and she also has to cook, shop for groceries, clean the house and take care of the children, I can tell you she is going to be too tired for sex. Husbands need to be aware of this.

If they want their wives' cooperation in the sexual relationship, they should make it their responsibility to help with the household chores. It is the wife's responsibility to keep the home and take care of the children, so she will feel like she needs to do those things. But if she is expected to work an outside job on top of all this, then the husband should be willing to help. If he will do this, she will have no excuse not to be ready to actively participate in the sexual relationship.

A Lack of Personal Hygiene

A lack of personal hygiene can hinder a good sex life. When a couple enters into the sex act, that is about as intimate or as close as one person can get to another. Both husband and wife should take care to practice good hygiene so that neither mate will be turned off when it comes time for the couple to come together.

Still another reason is, if a person has been sexually active before marriage, sometimes those experiences can keep him or her from enjoying the sexual experience they have with their spouses. In other words, they had a specific experience with someone before marriage and they expect the same experience with their mates. This is an area where open communication is extremely important.

It is important to not be offended if a mate may not want to be involved in certain sexual techniques. A husband or wife should not take a spouse's refusal as a put-down. There are all kinds of things that people do to enhance their sexual life. Some of those things are right, and some of them are wrong. Just because a spouse wants to perform an act does not mean that a partner has to be in accord with it — or should be — especially if what that spouse wants to do goes against the Word of God. No spouse should put anything off on the mate if he or she is not in agreement. There is a way in the Lord that every married couple can have a good sexual life without doing things that are considered abnormal.

One more reason a married couple may not enjoy a good sex life is that the husband and wife do not plan their time together. My husband and I learned that you need to plan a time that is good for both parties. Your intimate time does not necessarily need to be spontaneous to be good. Some mates may not feel that it can be anything but spontaneous because they never have tried having their intimate time any other way. But if they would take time to plan, chances are the wife, or maybe even the husband, would be more responsive and their time together would be very enjoyable.

My husband and I plan our times, and it is almost like having a date, so we look forward to being together. Once in a while, something may come up, or we may have too much going on to keep our date, so we communicate that and reschedule. This way, neither of us is upset if we do not get together at a certain time.

The fact you can reschedule does not mean you can keep putting off your spouse due to tiredness, or because you do not feel like being intimate. The Word tells us what to do as husbands and wives — not to deprive one another. Even when you do not feel like being intimat e, or you may be too tired, you can enter into the relationship by faith, and before it is all over, you will have thoroughly enjoyed it. Although you may not feel like having sex at the start, if you begin it by faith, the feelings will manifest.

7

The Witnessing Lifestyle

When Adam ate from the tree of the knowledge of good and evil, he sinned against God and this sin of disobedience cut him off from the Lord. We can see this is true because we know from Genesis 3:8–10, that God used to walk in the garden in the cool of the day and talk with Adam. But then, in Genesis 3:24, the Bible says Adam was driven out of the garden because of his disobedience.

Since we come from Adam, we have all inherited Adam's sin nature. So we, too, are cut off from God just as Adam was. We are not able to enjoy fellowship with Him as Adam once did in the garden — until we agree to God's plan of salvation by accepting His Son Jesus Christ as our personal Savior and Lord.

Second Corinthians 5:18 tells us that, as born-again Believers, our relationship with God is restored through our acceptance of Jesus Christ as Savior and Lord. We are no longer cut off from God. This Scripture says:

**Now all things are of God, who has reconciled us
to Himself through Jesus Christ, and has given us the
ministry of reconciliation.**

To reconcile means "to bring together, to restore." We
see from this Scripture that God restored us to Himself
through Jesus, and then gave us the work of bringing others
to Him through Jesus Christ.

So, the ministry of reconciliation is our God-given responsibility—each and every one of us, as children of God,
has this calling. The ministry of reconciliation was not given
just to the leaders or ministry gifts Jesus has placed in His
Church. We are all responsible for helping to bring those
still lost into the Kingdom of God. And we must be about
out Father's business. We cannot be ashamed of the Gospel
of Christ because God's Word says **it is the power of God to
salvation for everyone who believes** (Romans 1:16). We should
be sharing Jesus with our families, friends, and neighbors. As
my husband says, "It is time for Christians to come out of
the closet!" Everyone else is out, so why are we still in? It is
up to us to win our communities for Christ.

We also should be living our lives in such a way as to be
a witness for Jesus. If we are always down and out, no one is
ever going to want to know the Lord we know. We may be
the only Jesus some will ever get to know before they die. Personally, I would not want to be responsible for anyone rejecting salvation because of my ugly actions and miserable
looks. The word *gospel* means *"Good News";* my life should
be that of a witness of the "good news" of Jesus Christ.

Our lives should be filled with the joy of the Lord. Joy is
a fruit of the spirit that is planted in us when we are born-
again (Galatians 5:22). Reconciliation — receiving Jesus as

personal Savior and Lord — gives us joy. Every one of us has joy already, regardless of how we feel. Jesus said in John 15:11:

"These things have I spoken to you, that My joy may remain in you, and that your joy may be full."

We have to believe we have joy, simply because Jesus says He has already given it to us. Many of us forget that we have to receive joy by faith — just as we have to receive everything else from God by faith. It is important to walk in joy because the joy of the Lord draws the attention of the world — it can even be contagious. The world wants the joy that can only be had in Christ, so they are likely to be open to sharing Jesus with them.

We need to consistently walk by faith, enjoying a victorious, overcoming Christian life. Faith is important in the ministry of reconciliation because it is what empowers us to have a blessed life. Walking in victory is another testimony of the "good news" of Jesus Christ that opens doors to people's lives. Before my husband and I ever began to walk by faith, no one ever sought our advice or opinion. But now we receive so many requests for advice and counseling that we simply cannot respond to all of them.

And it goes without saying that we need to walk in love. Matthew 22:37–39 tells us that there is no greater commandment than to love God and to love your neighbor as yourself. You are supposed to love God, others and yourself. If you don't love yourself, then you are probably going to have a challenge loving other people. And since you must love other people, then you need to love yourself.

In John 13:35, Jesus told His disciples that it was by their love that people would know they were His disciples.

Our love should set us apart from the world; it should iden-
tify us as belonging to Christ. So many people want so des-
perately to be different, and here is a way that they can be
different. When you walk in love, people notice you. In fact,
they are attracted to you. Love will open doors into people's
lives so that you can share Jesus with them.

You can love for the same reason you can walk by faith
and walk in joy — because the love of God has been poured
out in your heart by the Holy Spirit (Romans 5:5). You have
love in you; you just have to choose to walk in it. When you
walk in love, with joy, and have victory in your life, the world
is going to see and want what you have — that is, Jesus!

I think it is really beautiful the way the Lord has seen
to it that every member of His Body has a part to play in
His salvation for the world. I think there is no greater honor
than the privilege of working together with the Lord to
bring His Word to a dying world. I hope that Christians
everywhere recognize the fact that they have been given the
ministry of reconciliation and determine to successfully fulfill this calling to the glory of God. I pray also that the
Body of Christ will not be ashamed of the Gospel of Jesus
Christ, but that they will share Jesus with their families,
friends, and their communities, and that their lives will be a
witness to the world of how truly wonderful it is to serve
the Lord.

My hope is that every member in the Body of Christ
will see how important his or her Christian walk is as an example before the world. We, as Jesus' representative in the
earth-realm, are witnesses and ambassadors for Him. Just
think: our actions can mean the difference between a person accepting or rejecting Christ, between having eternal
life or eternal damnation. Certainly, no one would want

another person to spend eternity cut off from God because of their actions.

I encourage you to think about how important your Christian walk is as an example before the world. Is doing what you want to do without regard to how your actions affect those around you worth someone else's eternal salvation? Think about it!

Determine to be an example of Jesus and then be sure to take every opportunity to minister the Lord when those you meet seek to have what God has so graciously given you — a personal relationship with Him through His Son, Jesus Christ. Remember also, that Proverbs 11:30 says: . . . **He who wins souls is wise.**

For a complete list of books and tapes by Drs. Frederick K.C. and Betty R. Price, please write

Drs. Fred and Betty Price
Crenshaw Christian Center
P.O. Box 90000
Los Angeles CA 90009

BOOKS BY BETTY R. PRICE, D.D.

STANDING BY GOD'S MAN

THROUGH THE FIRE & THROUGH THE WATER
My Triumph Over Cancer

BOOKS BY FREDERICK K.C. PRICE, PH.D.

HOW FAITH WORKS

IS HEALING FOR ALL?

HOW TO OBTAIN STRONG FAITH
Six Principles

NOW FAITH IS

THE HOLY SPIRIT—
The Missing Ingredient

FAITH, FOOLISHNESS, OR PRESUMPTION?

THANK GOD FOR EVERYTHING?

HOW TO BELIEVE GOD FOR A MATE

LIVING IN THE REALM OF THE SPIRIT

THE ORIGIN OF SATAN

CONCERNING THOSE WHO HAVE FALLEN
ASLEEP

HOMOSEXUALITY:
State of Birth or State of Mind?

WALKING IN GOD'S WORD
Through His Promises

PRACTICAL SUGGESTIONS FOR SUCCESSFUL
MINISTRY

NAME IT AND CLAIM IT!
The Power of Positive Confession

THE VICTORIOUS, OVERCOMING LIFE
(A Verse-by-Verse Study on the Book of Colossians)

A NEW LAW FOR A NEW PEOPLE

THE PROMISED LAND
(A New Era for the Body of Christ)

THREE KEYS TO POSITIVE CONFESSION

THE WAY, THE WALK, AND THE WARFARE OF
THE BELIEVER
(A Verse-by-Verse Study on the Book of Ephesians)

BEWARE! THE LIES OF SATAN

TESTING THE SPIRITS

IDENTIFIED WITH CHRIST:
A Complete Cycle From Defeat to Victory

THE CHRISTIAN FAMILY:
Practical Insight for Family Living
(formerly MARRIAGE AND THE FAMILY)

THE HOLY SPIRIT:

THE HELPER WE ALL NEED

FIVE LITTLE FOXES OF FAITH

BUILDING ON A FIRM FOUNDATION

DR. PRICE'S GOLDEN NUGGETS
A Treasury of Wisdom for Both Ministers and Laypeople

LIVING IN HOSTILE TERRITORY
A Survival Guide for the Overcoming Christian

THE TRUTH ABOUT . . . BOOK SERIES

About the Author

Dr. Betty R. Price, the wife of Dr. Frederick K.C. Price, is an ordained minister and serves as a pastoral assistant at Crenshaw Christian Center. She is often a guest speaker at church retreats and seminars, ministering to the needs of women from every walk of life. Her book, *Through the Fire & Through the Water,* documents her struggle and triumph over cancer, while *Standing by God's Man* chronicles her life with Dr. Price and the early years of Crenshaw Christian Center. Dr. Betty founded the church's women's fellowship, the intercessory prayer network, as well as the alcohol and drug abuse and community outreach programs.